Celebrating Hockey's History

The Original 6

NEW YORK RANGERS

Eric Zweig

Crabtree Publishing Company

www.crabtreebooks.com

Celebrating
Hockey's
History
The Original 6

Author: Eric Zweig,
  Member of the Society for International
  Hockey Research

Editor: Ellen Rodger

Editorial director: Kathy Middleton

Design: Tammy McGarr

Photo research: Tammy McGarr

Proofreader: Wendy Scavuzzo

**Production coordinator and
  Prepress technician:** Tammy McGarr

Print coordinator: Margaret Amy Salter

Photo Credits:

AP Images: Tom Sande, p 7; Marty Lederhandler, p 11 (right middle);
  Ron Frehm, pp 13 (bottom right), 23; ASSOCIATED PRESS, p 20;
  Paul J. Bereswill, p 27 (bottom)
Getty Images: New York Times Co. p 9; New York Daily News Archive,
  p 21; Bill Wippert, p 25 (top)
Hockey Gods: p 5 (bottom)
Hockey Hall of Fame: p 10; Lewis Portnoy, p 12; Le Studio du Hockey,
  p 13 (top left); Dave Sandford, p 15 (top left); Graphic Artists, p 15 (right
  middle); Turofsky, pp 16, 22; O - Pee-Chee, p 19 (right middle)
Keystone: © Kostas Lymperopoulos, front cover, title page; © Bildbyran,
  p 6; © Kostas Lymperopoulos, p26; © Duncan Williams, p 27
Library of Congress: George Grantham Bain, pp 5 (top right), 28 (inset)
Shutterstock: © Kyle Besler, p 25 (bottom); © spatuletail, p 29 (top right)
Wikimedia: public domain, pp 4, 15 (bottom left), 18; Alex Goykhman,
  p 8; creative commons, pp 11 (bottom left), 28–29 (top); Lisa Gansky,
  p 14; Michael Miller, p 19 (top right)

Library and Archives Canada Cataloguing in Publication

Zweig, Eric, 1963-, author
    New York Rangers / Eric Zweig.

(The original six : celebrating hockey's history)
Includes index.
Issued in print and electronic formats.
ISBN 978-0-7787-3440-6 (hardcover).--
ISBN 978-0-7787-3465-9 (softcover).--
ISBN 978-1-4271-1925-4 (HTML)

    1. New York Rangers (Hockey team)--Juvenile literature.
2. New York Rangers (Hockey team)--History--Juvenile literature.
I. Title.

GV848.N45Z84 2017   j796.962'64097471   C2017-903483-9
                                                C2017-903484-7

Library of Congress Cataloging-in-Publication Data

Names: Zweig, Eric, 1963- author.
Title: New York Rangers / Eric Zweig.
Description: New York : Crabtree Publishing Company, [2018] |
  Series: The Original Six: Celebrating hockey's history | Includes index.
  | Audience: Ages: 10-14. | Audience: Grades: 7 to 8.
Identifiers: LCCN 2017029658 (print) | LCCN 2017037591 (ebook) |
  ISBN 9781427119254 (Electronic HTML) |
  ISBN 9780778734406 (Reinforced library binding) |
  ISBN 9780778734659 (Paperback)
Subjects: LCSH: New York Rangers (Hockey team)--History--Juvenile
  literature.
Classification: LCC GV848.N43 (ebook) |
  LCC GV848.N43 Z94 2018 (print) | DDC 796.962/64097471--dc23
LC record available at https://lccn.loc.gov/2017029658

Crabtree Publishing Company
www.crabtreebooks.com   1-800-387-7650

Printed in the USA/102017/CG20170907

**Published in Canada
Crabtree Publishing**
616 Welland Ave.
St. Catharines, Ontario
L2M 5V6

**Published in the United States
Crabtree Publishing**
PMB 59051
350 Fifth Avenue, 59th Floor
New York, New York 10118

**Published in the United Kingdom
Crabtree Publishing**
Maritime House
Basin Road North, Hove
BN41 1WR

**Published in Australia
Crabtree Publishing**
3 Charles Street
Coburg North
VIC, 3058

Table of Contents

The Original 6

Celebrating Hockey's History

NEW YORK HOCKEY HISTORY

Hockey history in New York City dates back to the late 1890s. An early American hockey league started up in New York in those days, too. The NHL came to the city in 1925, although the Rangers didn't come onboard until 1926.

Ice Palace Team

During the winter of 1895–96, a hockey team made up of Canadians living in New York City practiced at a rink called the Ice Palace and played a few games against visiting teams. They were the first hockey team in New York. At the end of that winter, in March 1896, a new arena opened in New York called the St. Nicholas Rink. It would be the heart of hockey in New York City until the NHL came to town.

St. Nicholas Hockey Club, 1905-1906

Local Amateur League

In November 1896, a league was formed with two teams in New York and two teams in Brooklyn. It was called the Amateur Hockey League of New York, but would become known as the American Amateur Hockey League after teams from other cities joined, too. This league lasted until 1916–17.

Tex's Rangers

When the NHL was formed in November 1917, it only had teams in Canadian cities. The NHL didn't expand into the United States until the 1924–25 season. There was talk of adding a New York team to the NHL that year. But instead, the Boston Bruins became the league's first American **franchise**. A year later, the New York Americans joined the NHL. They rented the ice at Madison Square Garden, and became such a hit that the Garden's owner decided he wanted his own team. His name was Tex Rickard, and it's said that Tex's team was called the Rangers because of a play on words with the famous lawmen known as the Texas Rangers. (That's how the baseball team got its name, too.) Hockey fans in New York quickly came to love the Rangers. They had a clean and skillful style, and they won the Stanley Cup for the first time in just their second season. No other expansion team since then has ever won a championship so quickly.

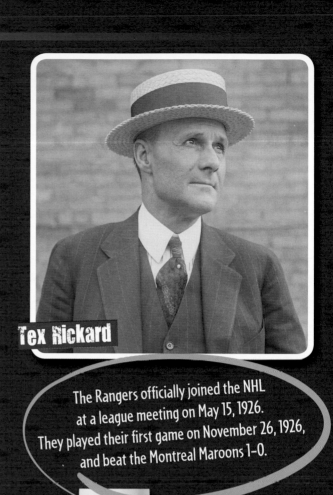

Tex Rickard

The Rangers officially joined the NHL at a league meeting on May 15, 1926. They played their first game on November 26, 1926, and beat the Montreal Maroons 1–0.

NEW YORK AMERICANS

New York Americans Jersey worn by Tommy Anderson in 1936

The New York Americans played the first NHL game in New York City on December 15, 1925. They lost 3-1 to the Montreal Canadiens.

THE NHL AT 100

With the addition of the Vegas Golden Knights in the 2017–18 season, the NHL celebrates its 100th birthday with 31 teams. From a low of just three teams in 1917–18, the NHL is now bigger than it's ever been!

The Original Four!

There never really was an "Original Six" in NHL history. The league actually began with four teams in 1917–18. When the Montreal Wanderers dropped out early that first season, only the Montreal Canadiens, Ottawa Senators, and Toronto Arenas were left. The NHL grew from just three teams to six teams by the 1924–25 season. It was up to 10 teams in 1926–27 when the New York Rangers entered the league.

Then There Were Six

In the early years, the NHL had two divisions: The Canadian Division (sometimes called the International Division) and the American Division. The Rangers finished in first place in the American Division in their very first season. They won the Stanley Cup three times in their first 13 years and reached the Stanley Cup Finals three other times. Many other teams were not as successful. Hard times during The Great Depression of the 1930s saw three teams go out of business. By the 1942–43 season, only the Rangers, Canadiens, Toronto Maple Leafs, Boston Bruins, Detroit Red Wings and Chicago Blackhawks were left. They were the only six teams in the NHL for the next 25 years.

Toronto Maple Leafs

Boston Bruins

New York Rangers

Detroit Red Wings

Montreal Canadiens

Chicago Black hawks
(now Blackhawks)

The furnace at Madison Square Garden in New York City was converted from oil to coal heat, in 1942. Not too proud to pitch in, several athletes lent a hand at shoveling coal. From left to right: boxers Joe Peralta and Chester Rico, and Rangers "Red" Garrett and Bryan Hextall.

Rangers' Lean Years

Those 25 years were mostly good for Toronto, Montreal, and Detroit, but the Rangers, Bruins, and Blackhawks all struggled. The Rangers missed the playoffs 18 times in the 25 seasons from 1942–43 through 1966–67. They were much better after NHL expansion in 1967, but it still took until 1994 before the Rangers finally won the Stanley Cup again. By then, it had been 54 years since their last cup victory in 1940.

Now There's a Record!

To date, no team in NHL history has ever gone as long as the Rangers between Stanley Cup victories—although a few have come close! Some people claim that the "hockey gods" cursed the Rangers when team officials burned the **mortgage** papers after paying off the loan on Madison Square Garden during the 1940–41 season. Other stories say that Red Dutton, the man who ran the New York Americans, put a curse on the Rangers when his team dropped out of the NHL after the 1941–42 season.

THE STANLEY CUP

The Rangers became the **first American-based NHL team** to **win** the **Stanley Cup** in **1928**. The first-ever American team to win it was the Seattle Metropolitans of the Pacific Coast Hockey Association in 1917.

The first all-American Stanley Cup Finals saw the **Rangers** face the **Boston Bruins** in **1929**. Boston won the best-of-three series in two straight.

Rangers coach Lester Patrick had to **take over** in net when **goalie Lorne Chabot** was **injured** during Game 2 of the 1928 **Stanley Cup Finals**. Lester led the Rangers to a 2-1 victory in overtime. (Teams didn't usually carry backup goalies back then.)

Alexander Karpovtsev, Alexei Kovalev, Sergei Nemchinov, and Sergei Zubov became the **first Russian players** to have their **names engraved on the Stanley Cup** when the Rangers won it in **1994**.

Greg Gilbert is the **only player in NHL history** to **win** the **Stanley Cup** with **two different New York teams**. He won with the Islanders in 1982 and 1983, and with the Rangers in 1994.

General cup info

The Stanley Cup is the oldest trophy in professional sports.

It was donated in 1892 by Sir Frederick Arthur Stanley, an English **lord**. Lord Stanley of Preston served as Canada's Sixth **Governor General** and became a hockey fan while in Canada.

The cup was originally a **"challenge cup"** for Canada's top amateur hockey clubs. It has been the top prize in the NHL since 1926.

Detachable rings

* When there is no longer any more space, the oldest ring is removed and retired. It stays at the Hockey Hall of Fame.
* A new ring is placed on the bottom for new winning teams and players.
* Winners' names remain on the cup for roughly 50 years before the ring is retired.

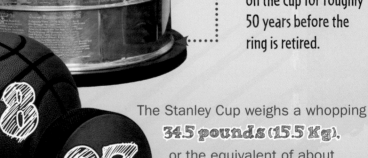

The Stanley Cup weighs a whopping **34.5 pounds (15.5 Kg)**, or the equivalent of about **93 pucks, or 28 basketballs**.

What a Circus!

The Rangers had to play all five games of the 1928 Stanley Cup Finals on the road in Montreal because of a circus at Madison Square Garden. Over the years, the annual circus often forced the Rangers to play on the road during the playoffs.

Tennis Anyone?

The 1932 Stanley Cup Finals, when the Toronto Maple Leafs swept the Rangers in a best-of-five series, is sometimes known as "the tennis series." The reason is because the scores of the games looked like the scores in a tennis match. The Leafs won 6-4, 6-2, 6-4.

Brothers in Arms

Two sets of brothers won the Stanley Cup with the Rangers in 1940: Mac and Neil Colville, and Lynn and Muzz Patrick. Lynn and Muzz had their names engraved on the Stanley Cup along with their father, Lester Patrick, who was the Rangers' general manager.

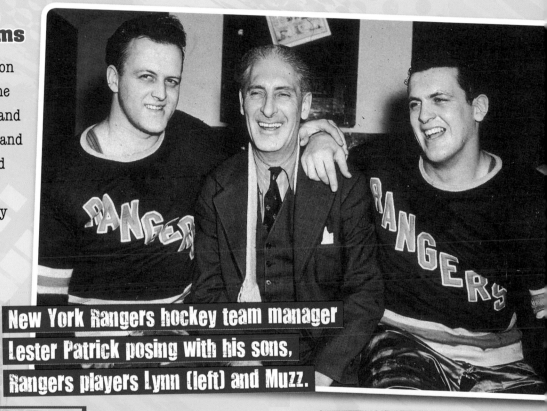

New York Rangers hockey team manager Lester Patrick posing with his sons, Rangers players Lynn (left) and Muzz.

Rangers' Winning Years

1928 over Montreal Maroons
1933 over Toronto Maple Leafs
1940 over Toronto Maple Leafs
1994 over Vancouver Canucks

Family Affair

Frank Boucher, who won the Stanley Cup as a player with the Rangers in 1928 and 1933, and as their coach in 1940, was the fourth member of his family to win it. His brother George won the cup with the Ottawa Senators in 1920, 1921, 1923, and 1927. His brothers Billy and Bobby both won it with the Montreal Canadiens in 1924.

Overtime *Over Time*

Seventeen players in NHL history have scored the Stanley Cup-winning goal in overtime. Bill Cook and Bryan Hextall did it for the Rangers in 1933 and 1940. Pete Babando (Detroit) and Alec Martinez (Los Angeles) beat the Rangers in overtime in 1950 and 2014.

STAR SCORERS

The Rangers haven't always been the NHL's best team, but they've boasted some of the league's best scorers and lines.

Fantastic Forward Line

Frank Boucher and the Cook Brothers sounds like a band name. But in the early days of the Rangers, the combination of Frank Boucher centering brothers Bill and Bun Cook was one of the first great forward lines in NHL history. Boucher was the playmaker, leading the team in assists nine times in the first 10 seasons, and topping the NHL three times. Bill Cook was the **sniper**, leading the team in goals six times and the league three times. He also led the NHL in points twice.

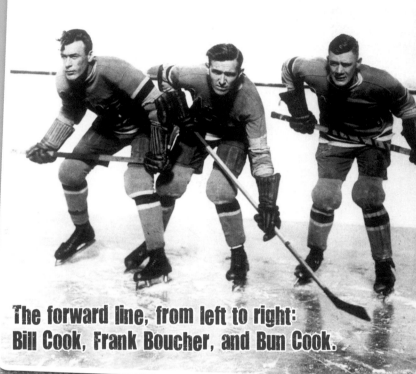

The forward line, from left to right: Bill Cook, Frank Boucher, and Bun Cook.

GAG Line

In the early 1970s, the Rangers trio of Jean Ratelle, Rod Gilbert, and Vic Hadfield was known as the GAG Line. This GAG didn't mean funny business. It stood for Goal-A-Game. During the 1971–72 season, Ratelle became the first Ranger to reach 100 points. Hadfield was the first player in team history to score 50 goals that year. Rod Gilbert would go on to become the team's all-time leader with 406 goals and 1,021 points.

Scoring Leader

Andy Bathgate never had a lot of great teammates around him, but he knew how to get the best out of them. Bathgate led the Rangers in assists for nine straight seasons from 1955 through 1964. He led the team in points for the first eight of those seasons. Bathgate tied Chicago's Bobby Hull for the NHL scoring lead with 84 points in 1961–62, but Hull was presented with the Art Ross Trophy because he had 50 goals that year and Bathgate only scored 28.

Cup Clincher

Mark Messier was a great scorer, but he was brought to the Rangers in 1991–92 for just one reason: to lead the team to the Stanley Cup. With the team trailing the New Jersey Devils three games to two in the 1994 Eastern Conference Finals, Messier guaranteed a victory in Game Six and then backed it up by scoring a **hat trick**. In Game Seven of the Stanley Cup Finals, Messier scored the cup-clinching goal against the Vancouver Canucks to deliver the championship.

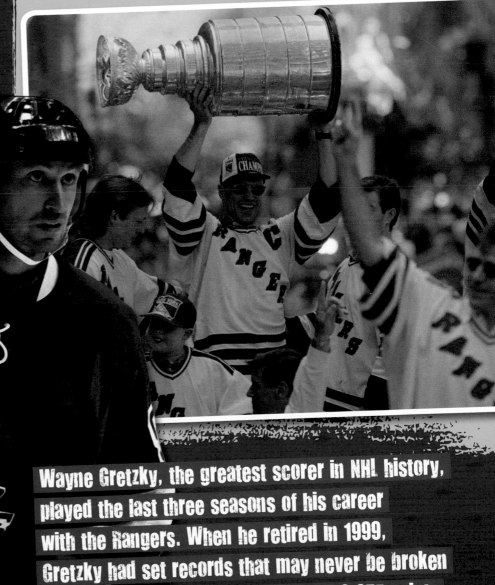

Wayne Gretzky, the greatest scorer in NHL history, played the last three seasons of his career with the Rangers. When he retired in 1999, Gretzky had set records that may never be broken with 894 goals and 1,963 assists for 2,857 points.

DOMINATING DEFENSEMEN

On a hockey team, it's the defense's main job to keep opponents from scoring. Good D players should also be skilled in defending the blue line in the other team's zone. And the Rangers have had some of the best blueliners in NHL history.

Brad Park

Many hockey experts consider Bobby Orr of the Boston Bruins to be the greatest hockey player of all time. So it's not surprising that pretty much everyone agrees that Orr was the best defenseman in the NHL during the early 1970s. The second-best was Brad Park of the Rangers. Park was a smooth skater who could steer opposition players away from the net in his own end of the rink, while scoring goals and setting up teammates in the other team's end. Park never won the Norris Trophy during his career, but he finished second in the voting six times! In 1975, the Rangers traded Park to Boston and he eventually ended up replacing Orr on the Bruins' blue line.

Harry Howell of the Rangers won the Norris Trophy as the NHL's best defenseman for the 1966–67 season. He was the last player to win the award before Bobby Orr won it eight years in a row!

Ching Johnson

Ching Johnson was an original Ranger in 1926–27. At 5-foot-11 (180 cm) and 210 pounds (95 kg), he was a huge player of this era and one of the game's hardest hitters. Johnson never added much to the offense, but it was always tough for the other team's forwards to get around him. There was no Norris Trophy back in his day, but when the NHL first began selecting All-Stars in 1930–31, Johnson earned two selections to the First Team and two to the Second Team in the first four seasons.

Brian Leetch

Brian Leetch scored 23 goals in his first full season with the Rangers in 1988–89. That set a record for a rookie defenseman which has never been matched. After that fast start, Leetch just kept getting better and better. During the 1991–92 season, he set career highs with 80 assists and 102 points to join Bobby Orr, Denis Potvin, Paul Coffey, and Al MacInnis as the only defensemen in NHL history to reach the 100-point plateau. Leetch won the Norris Trophy that year, and won it again in 1996–97. In 1994, he helped the Rangers win the Stanley Cup and became the first American-born player in history to win the Conn Smythe Trophy as playoff MVP.

GREAT GOALIES

Henrik Lundqvist is one of the best goalies in the world today. He's won more games than any goalie in Rangers history, but many others have had success, too.

King Henrik

Henrik Lundqvist grew up in a small town in Sweden. Most people there were skiers. Even his father was a ski instructor. But Henrik and his twin brother Joel loved hockey. Both brothers made it to the NHL, but only Henrik has become a superstar. In New York, they call him King Henrik. He joined the Rangers in 2006–07 and became the first goalie in NHL history to win 30 games or more in each of his first seven seasons. That streak would still be going if not for a **lockout** that shortened the 2012–13 season. Lundqvist won the Vezina Trophy as the league's best goaltender in 2011–12, and set the Rangers record for most career wins late in the 2013–14 season. On February 11, 2017, he became the 12th goalie in NHL history to win 400 games. Lundqvist reached the milestone in fewer games (727) than any other goalie. Ever.

Mike Richter

Mike Richter played his entire 14-year career with the Rangers from 1989 to 2003. Before Henrik Lundqvist, he held the team record with 301 wins. Richter still holds the team's single-season record with 42 wins, which he set in 1993-94. Even more importantly, he posted all 16 wins the Rangers needed to claim the Stanley Cup that spring to end the team's 54-year championship drought.

Ed Giacomin

When Ed Giacomin was 15 years old, a scout at a junior tryout camp for the Detroit Red Wings told him he'd never make it to the NHL. But Giacomin didn't give up. He eventually toiled for six full seasons in the minors before reaching the NHL with the Rangers in 1965. He played more games than any other goalie in the league from 1966 through 1970. In 1970-71, he combined with teammate Gilles Villemure to win the Vezina Trophy, which no other Ranger goalie had won since Dave Kerr all the way back in 1939-40.

Chuck Rayner

Chuck Rayner of the Rangers became just the second goalie in NHL history to win the Hart Trophy as league MVP in 1949-50. The only other goalies to win it were Roy Worters (1928-29), Al Rollins (1953-54), Jacques Plante (1961-62), Dominik Hasek (1996-97, 1997-98), José Théodore (2001-02) and Carey Price (2014-15).

RANGERS RECORDS

Like most NHL teams of the Original Six era, the Rangers have a storied past and some impressive records.

Put That in Your Hat!

Bill Cook holds the Rangers all-time record with **11 hat tricks**. He scored three goals in a game 10 times and four goals in a game once.

11

Numbers Game

5 **GOALS** in one game by Don Murdoch on October 12, 1976 and Mark Pavelich on February 23, 1983.

5 **ASSISTS** in one game by five different players: Walt Tkaczuk, Rod Gilbert (three times), Don Maloney, Brian Leetch, and Wayne Gretzky.

7 **POINTS** in one game by Steve Vickers (3 goals, 4 assists) on February 18, 1976.

12 **GOALS** by the team in a 12-1 win over the California Golden Seals on November 21, 1971. The team record for most goals in a shutout victory is a 10-0 win over the Seals on November 17, 1974.

59 **SAVES** in one game by Mike Richter on January 31, 1991.

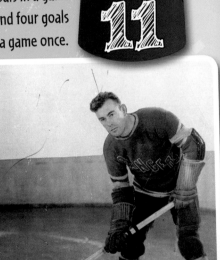

Bill Cook

Rangers Regular-Season Franchise Leaders (Career)

Games	Goals	Assists	Points	Wins	Shutouts	Goals-Against Average
1,160	406	741	1,021	405*	61*	1.61
Harry Howell	Rod Gilbert	Brian Leetch	Rod Gilbert	Henrik Lundqvist	Henrik Lundqvist	Lorne Chabot

* still active entering 2017–18

Hanging in the Rafters

A retired number is a jersey that has been taken out of **circulation** by a team to honor the player who wore the number. The jersey numbers are often hung in the rafters so fans can see them. These numbers have all been retired by the New York Rangers.

Ed Giacomin (1965–75)	Brian Leetch (1987–2004)	Harry Howell (1952–69)	Rod Gilbert (1960–77)	Andy Bathgate (1952–64)	Adam Graves (1991–2001)	Mark Messier (1991–97, 2000–04)	Jean Ratelle (1960–76)	Mike Richter (1989–2003)
1	2	3	7	9	9	11	19	35

Winning Streak

The longest winning streak in Rangers history is 10 games, which they have accomplished twice. Once during the 1939–40 season and once in 1972–73. The longest scoring streak in Rangers history is also 10 games. Andy Bathgate scored in 10 straight games (11 goals in total) during the 1962–63 season.

Team Record

The Rangers set team records with **53 wins** and **113 points** in 2014-15. They had **52 wins** and **112 points** in 1993-94.

Rangers Franchise Leaders (Season)

Goals	Assists	Points	Wins	Shutouts	Goals-Against Average
54	80	123	42	13	1.41
Jaromir Jagr (2005–06)	Brian Leetch (1991–92)	Jaromir Jagr (2005–06)	Mike Richter (1993–94)	John Ross Roach (1928–29)	John Ross Roach (1928–29)

THE BROADWAY BLUESHIRTS

The Rangers are sometimes known as The Broadway Blueshirts. They've been wearing blue as their main color since they started in the NHL back in 1926–27.

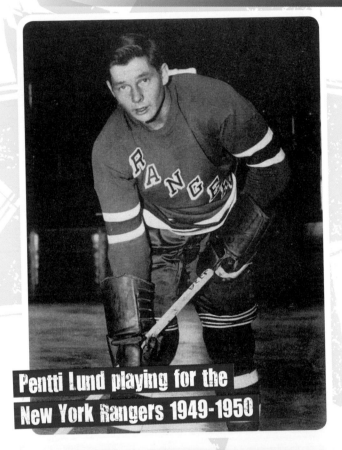

Pentti Lund playing for the New York Rangers 1949-1950

Patriotic Uniforms

When the New York Americans became the first NHL team in New York in 1925–26, they wore red, white, and blue uniforms with stars and stripes. The uniforms looked a lot like an American flag. When the Rangers entered the NHL, they also chose red, white, and blue as their colors, but their uniforms weren't as flashy as the Americans. The Rangers wore a mainly blue sweater with a red band and two white stripes on the sleeves and at the waist. The word RANGERS was written diagonally down the front. The blue on their sweaters and socks was also a slightly lighter color in the earlier years than it would become. But essentially, the Rangers uniforms have changed very little throughout the team's history.

Fancy Pants

An old newspaper story from Toronto in 1929 says that all hockey pants used to be white. Then black pants were introduced, and later khaki. The story says that the Toronto Maple Leafs started wearing blue pants during the 1928–29 season. Then the Rangers, not to be out-kitted, introduced red pants in 1929–30. However, according to some sources, Detroit actually was the first team to introduce colorful hockey pants when they wore red pants in 1927–28.

Lady Liberty on a Hockey Jersey?

A white version of the sweaters and socks, with blue and red stripes, was first introduced in 1951–52. For a brief time in the 1970s, the Rangers wore a crest on their chest that said NEW YORK across the top, and had RANGERS in smaller diagonal letters. During the late 1990s and into the early 2000s, the Rangers sometimes wore darker blue sweaters with a logo featuring a designed based on New York's famous Statue of Liberty.

New York Rangers goaltender Henrik Lundqvist's mask featuring the Statue of Liberty.

The first hockey skates were blades attached separately to boots. Today's skates are marvels of lightweight engineering technology that are meant to make players feel there is no blade attached to the bottom of their feet.

Caught Red, White, and Blue Handed

According to a booklet about uniform history written for the NHL in 2007, the Rangers became the first team to wear colored gloves. They ditched the natural, buff-colored leather gloves worn by all pro teams in 1957, and donned slick red, white, and blue gloves. The Leafs followed suit and began wearing blue gloves during the 1958–59 season. Detroit was the last team to jump on the colored gloves bandwagon in 1967–68.

TROPHY WINNERS

There's nothing in hockey to match the excitement of winning the Stanley Cup. Still, the NHL's collection of individual trophies is pretty impressive. Here's a look at some of the Rangers who've taken home the hardware.

Goalie Goals

From its beginning in 1926–27 through the 1980–81 season, the Vezina Trophy for best goalie was presented to the goalie (or goalies) on the team that allowed the fewest goals. Since the 1981–82 season, the Vezina has gone to the goalie who has been voted to be the best in the NHL. That same season, a new trophy was donated to the NHL to honor the goalies on the team that gives up the fewest goals. It's known as the Jennings Trophy. It's named after William Jennings, who was the longtime president of the New York Rangers. To date, no Rangers goalies have ever won the Jennings Trophy.

Rangers Frank Boucher with the Weber and Heilbroner Trophy, given to the team's highest scorer in 1930.

Other Rangers who won the Lady Byng Trophy

1938–39	Clint Smith
1947–48	Buddy O'Connor
1949–50	Edgar Laprade
1956–57	Andy Hebenton
1957–58	Camille Henry
1971–72	Jean Ratelle
1998–99	Wayne Gretzky

What a Sport!

Frank Boucher won the Lady Byng Trophy for sportsmanship seven times! He won it for four straight seasons from 1927 to 1931 and then three more times from 1932 through 1935. He was such a gentleman player, Boucher was given the original trophy to keep and a new one was donated in 1936.

Jean Ratelle,
Lady Byng, 1972

NHL award winners show their trophies in 1972: Hawks' Tony Esposito, Vezina Trophy; Rangers' Jean Ratelle, Lady Byng Trophy; Bruins' Bobby Orr, Hart Trophy and Norris Trophy; and Canadiens' Ken Dryden, Calder Memorial Trophy.

Points Toppers

The two Rangers who led the NHL in points both did so before the Art Ross Trophy was donated to the NHL in 1948. **Bill Cook** led in the years 1926–27, 1932–33, and **Bryan Hextall** led in 1941–42.

Goal Leaders

Three Rangers led the NHL in goal-scoring before the Maurice "Rocket" Richard Trophy was donated to the NHL in 1999. **Bill Cook** led the league in 1926–27, 1931–32, 1932–33; **Bryan Hextall** led in 1939–40, 1940–41; and **Lynn Patrick** led in 1941–42.

Ranger Calder Memorial Trophy Winners

(NHL Rookie of the Year)

1939–40	Kilby MacDonald	1952–53	Lorne Worsley
1941–42	Grant Warwick	1953–54	Camille Henry
1945–46	Edgar Laprade	1972–73	Steve Vickers
1948–49	Pentti Lunde	1988–89	Brian Leetch

Rangers who have won the Hart Trophy as NHL MVP

1947–48	Buddy O'Connor
1949–50	Chuck Rayner
1958–59	Andy Bathgate
1991–92	Mark Messier

BEHIND THE BENCH

The Rangers have had some legendary men running their team and franchise over the years, including a former boxing promoter and **saloon** owner who founded the team. Several coaches spent their entire careers with the Rangers, and some went from player to coach with varying degrees of success.

Master Promoter

The Rangers' first owner was a scrappy survivor who knew how to make a buck. Tex Rickard was reportedly a cowboy while still a kid, then a Texas marshal, a Klondike gold prospector, and a saloon owner before he turned his hand to promoting boxing matches and owning a **fledgling** hockey franchise. Rickard died in 1929, three years after his team entered the league and just a year after they won their first Stanley Cup. His legacy includes the team's name, the Rangers, which was a play on Rickard's nickname Tex, and his years spent as a marshal.

First Coach

The first man hired as coach and general manager of the New York Rangers was Conn Smythe. He put together a great team, but he didn't get along with his bosses. Smythe was fired before the 1926–27 season even started and returned home to Toronto where he went on to great success as the boss of the Maple Leafs. Lester Patrick took over in New York and guided the Rangers to great success, too.

Les Patrick

Lester Patrick had been a star player in the early days of pro hockey before the NHL was formed. He won the Stanley Cup as a player with the Montreal Wanderers in 1906 and 1907.

Stanley Cup Final victory on April 13, 1940

In 1911, Lester and his brother Frank created the Pacific Coast Hockey Association (PCHA). Lester was a player, coach, general manager, and owner of the PCHA team in Victoria, British Columbia, and won the Stanley Cup with them in 1925. Lester led the Rangers to the Stanley Cup in their second season of 1927–28 and won it again in 1932–33. He was both coach and general manager of the team in those days, but was serving only as general manager when the Rangers won the cup again in 1939–40.

Frank Boucher

Frank Boucher had been a star player under Lester Patrick, and took over from him as coach in 1939 and as general manager in 1946. Patrick and Boucher are the only men to have won the Stanley Cup three times as members of the Rangers.

Emile Francis

Emile Francis served as both coach and general manager of the Rangers from 1965 to 1974. He coached and won more games than anyone else in franchise history, but never won the Stanley Cup.

Mike Keenan

Mike Keenan only spent one season as coach of the New York Rangers, but it was a good one! He led the Rangers to the Stanley Cup in 1993-94.

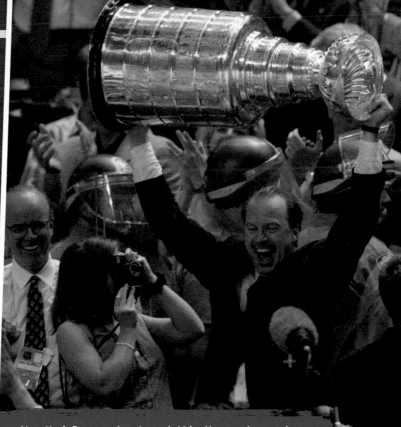

New York Rangers head coach Mike Keenan hoists the Stanley Cup in 1994 after his team defeated the Vancouver Canucks in the Stanley Cup finals at New York's Madison Square Garden. It was the Rangers first cup win in 54 years.

Glen Sather

From 1980 until 2015, Glen Sather served as a general manager with the Edmonton Oilers and New York Rangers for 2,700 regular-season games. He earned more wins (1,319) than anyone in NHL history.

Rangers Coaching Leaders

	Seasons	Games	Record	Stanley Cups
Emile Francis	1965-74	654	342-209-103	0
Lester Patrick	1926-39	604	281-216-107	2
Frank Boucher	1939-48, 1954	527	181-263-83	1
Alain Vigneault*	2013 to date	328	192-108-28	0
Tom Renney	2003-08	327	164-117-46	0

* still active

RANGERS BITS AND PIECES

In the NHL, the points system determines all. Players are awarded points for each goal or assist.

WHAT'S IN A NAME?

Hockey is famous for nicknames. Players give each other nicknames based on attributes such as height, hair color, or playing ability. Often they just shorten a last name. Some of the best Ranger's nickname are based on names and skills.

Frederick Joseph Cook "Bun"

What's Behind It: According to stories, the Hall-of-Famer was called Bun because a sportswriter once said that he was "quick as a bunny." But his wife always said that brother Bill started calling him "Bun" as a boy because he had a big nose.

Samuel James Henry "Sugar Jim"

What's Behind It: You would think that a guy nicknamed Sugar would either be sweet or have some sweet moves on the ice. But Rangers goalie (1941–42, 1945–48) Jim Henry apparently got the nickname as a child because of his love for the sweet stuff—candy.

Steve Buzinski "The Puck Goes Inski"

What's Behind It: Steve Buzinski played just nine games for the Rangers during the 1942–43 season. He had a record of 2–6–1 and allowed 55 goals in 560 minutes of playing time for a goals-against average of 5.89. Over the years, he's become known as "Steve Buzinski, the Puck-Goes-Inski."

Frank Boucher "Raffles"

What's Behind It: Francois Xavier Boucher won the Lady Byng Trophy for most gentlemanly player seven times in eight years in his 13 seasons with the Rangers (1926–1944). His nickname, earned for his puck-stealing abilities, came from a character in a book who was a "gentleman thief."

Honorable mentions

Rick "Nifty" Middleton · Camille "The Eel" Henry

6 Rangers have topped 100 points in a single season

Season	Player	Points
2005–06	Jaromir Jagr	123
1971–72	Jean Ratelle	109
1991–92	Mark Messier	107
1971–72	Vic Hadfield	106
1981–82	Mike Rogers	103
1991–92	Brian Leetch	102

3 Rangers have topped 50 points in a single season

Season	Player	Points
2005–06	Jaromir Jagr	54
1993–94	Adam Graves	52
1971–72	Vic Hadfield	50

The Rangers are sometimes called the Broadway Blueshirts.

Fast Starter

Ranger Derek Stepan tied a modern NHL record when he scored three goals in his first NHL game on October 9, 2010. The record was broken when Toronto's Auston Matthews scored four goals in his first game on October 12, 2016.

Derek Stepan, #21 of the New York Rangers, holds the three pucks he used to score a hat trick in his first NHL game.

Rangers' Firsts

BACK-TO-BACK Henrik Lundqvist is the only goalie in NHL history to appear in an Olympic gold medal game and the Stanley Cup Finals in the same year (2014). Unfortunately for Lundqvist, Sweden lost to Canada and the Rangers lost to Los Angeles.

SHUTOUT SHOUTOUT Hal Winkler, goalie for the Rangers, became the first rookie in NHL history to get a shutout in his first game when he led the Rangers to a 1-0 victory over the Montreal Maroons in the team's very first game on November 16, 1926.

FIRST GAME FINESSE Lorne Chabot of the Rangers became the first rookie in NHL history to get a shutout in his first playoff game when the Rangers tied the Boston Bruins 0-0 on April 2, 1927. (Playoff games sometimes ended in ties back then.)

BACK-TO-BACK The Rangers set an unusual NHL record when they opened the 1997–98 season by playing four consecutive tie games. This was before shootouts were used to break a tie at the end of overtime.

RIVALRIES

New York is the biggest city in North America. It has teams in all the major sports, and usually more than one in each league. The Rangers currently have an inner-city rivalry with the New York Islanders, and the New Jersey Devils are only a few miles away.

Americans

The New York Rangers didn't just share a city with the New York Americans, they also shared an arena. The bosses who owned Madison Square Garden also owned the Rangers. That was a big advantage for the team, who always seemed to have more money to spend than the cash-strapped Americans. Even though the Americans joined the NHL one year earlier, the Rangers quickly became a powerhouse in the NHL, while the Americans usually struggled just to make the playoffs. To try to create their own unique identity, the Americans renamed themselves the Brooklyn Americans in 1941–42—but they still played in New York at Madison Square Garden. The Americans had their worst year ever that season, and dropped out of the NHL.

New York, New York

The Rangers had the city to themselves for hockey for 30 years until the New York Islanders were formed in 1972–73. The Islanders were terrible that season, posting one of the worst records in NHL history with a mark of 12–60–6. Playing out in the suburbs of Long Island, the Islanders never got the same attention as the Rangers, but they improved quickly. The Islanders won the Stanley Cup four years in a row, starting with the 1979–80 season. The Rangers hadn't won the cup since 1940, and Islanders fans taunted them by chanting "1940!" whenever the two teams met.

Dealing with the Devils

When the New Jersey Devils entered the NHL in 1974–75, the team was based in Kansas City and was known as the Scouts. They lasted just two years there before spending the next six years in Denver as the Colorado Rockies. The team arrived in New Jersey in 1982–83 and has played in the same division as the Rangers and Islanders every year since. Devils fans hate the Rangers, and games between the two teams are always a battle!

Bad Blood with Boston

The Rangers have played more games against the Bruins than any other NHL team. Fans in New York and Boston don't like each other much, either, whether it's the Yankees and Red Sox, the Knicks and Celtics, the Patriots and the Jets, or the Rangers and Bruins.

ON HOME ICE

Madison Square Garden is known as "The World's Most Famous Arena." The truth is, that since 1879, there have been four different buildings known as Madison Square Garden. The Rangers have played in two of them.

1st Madison Square Garden

Six-Day Bike Race, 1908

Fast Facts

- Located at the corner of Madison Avenue and 26th Street, near Madison Square.
- Leased to bandleader Patrick S. Gilmore and renamed "Gilmore's Garden."
- Officially renamed Madison Square Garden on May 31, 1879.
- Demolished in 1889.
- **The Hippo-what?**
  Originally built in 1874 by the legendary circus showman P.T. Barnum, the building was known as "Barnum's Monster Classical and Geological **Hippodrome**."

2nd Madison Square Garden

Fast Facts

- Constructed on the same site as the original, opening on June 16, 1890.
- Sports events were mainly boxing and wrestling, indoor bicycle races, and horse shows.
- Hosted many political events.
- 8,000-seat arena
- Closed on May 5, 1925, and was demolished to make room for the New York Life Insurance Building that still stands at 51 Madison Avenue.

Madison Square Garden during the first hockey game after the completion of the first stage of the transformation. The game took place on October 27, 2011, between the New York Rangers and the Toronto Maple Leafs.

MADISON SQUARE GARDEN

4th Madison Square Garden

Fast Facts

- Officially opened on February 11, 1968, with a gala hosted by Hollywood stars Bob Hope and Bing Crosby.

- First Rangers game was a 3-1 win over the Philadelphia Flyers on February 18, 1968.

- Different sources show the cost of construction ranging between $43 million and $123 million. That would be equivalent to about $200 million to $830 million today.

- Underwent major modernizing renovations from 1989 to 1991 and from 2011 to 2013 (which cost about $1 billion!).

- Currently holds 18,006 for hockey; 18,500 for wrestling; 19,812 for basketball; 20,000 for concerts, and 20,789 for boxing.

3rd Madison Square Garden

Fast Facts

- Opened at 49th Street and 8th Avenue on November 24, 1925.

- Home of the New York Americans and New York Rangers in the NHL and New York Knicks of the NBA.

- Also hosted boxing, wrestling, track-and-field, college basketball, circuses, concerts and political events.

- Seating capacity of 18,000.

- Closed in 1968. Final Rangers game was a 3-3 tie with Detroit on February 11, 1968. Final event was the Westminster Kennel Club Dog Show on February 12–13, 1968.

- An office building and apartment complex has stood on the site since 1989.

Glossary

Challenge Cup An era in Stanley Cup history when there was no formal playoff season and the winner held the cup until another team challenged them for it

circulation Availability

fledgling New or just starting

franchise A team granted a right or license to play in the league

Governor General The head of state in Canada

hat tricks Three goals or points scored by one player during one game

hippodrome A theater or other performance venue

lockout When players are locked out or prevented from playing by team owners during a work or contract disagreement

lord A British nobleman

mortgage A loan for a property

saloon A bar

sniper A fast, accurate shot

Further Reading

If you're a fan of the New York Rangers, you may enjoy these books:

The Big Book of Hockey for Kids by Eric Zweig. Scholastic Canada, 2017.

The Home Team: New York Rangers by Holly Preston. Always Books Ltd., 2015.

The Screech Owls series by Roy MacGregor.

The Ultimate Book of Hockey Trivia for Kids by Eric Zweig. Scholastic Canada, 2015.

Websites to Check Out

The Hockey Hall of Fame: **www.hhof.com**

The New York Rangers website: **www.nhl.com/rangers**

NHL Uniforms Database: **www.nhluniforms.com**

The official National Hockey League website: **www.nhl.com**

Test Your Rangers' Knowledge

1. Which NHL team played in New York before the Rangers?

a) New York Americans
b) Montreal Maroons
c) New York Islanders
d) New York Jets

2. Who holds the Rangers' record for most points in a single season?

a) Rod Gilbert
b) Mark Messier
c) Camille Henry
d) Jaromir Jagr

3. Which of these players was not a member of the Rangers GAG Line?

a) Andy Bathgate
b) Rod Gilbert
c) Vic Hadfield
d) Jean Ratelle

4. Which NHL trophy was Brian Leetch the first American to win?

a) Norris Trophy
b) Art Ross Trophy
c) Conn Smythe Trophy
d) Selke Trophy

5. Which country is Henrik Lundqvist from?

a) Norway
b) Sweden
c) Finland
d) Denmark

1. a) New York Americans, 2. d) Jaromir Jagr; 3. a) Andy Bathgate 4. c) Conn Smythe Trophy; 5. d) Sweden

Places to Go

If you're ever in Toronto, be sure to visit the Hockey Hall of Fame. If you're in New York, you can see a game at Madison Square Garden or check out all sorts of other teams who play close by. If you're looking for hockey merchandise, check out the NHL Store in the heart of Manhattan.

About the Author

By the age of 10, Eric Zweig was already a budding sports fanatic who was filling his school news books with game reports instead of current events. He has been writing professionally about sports and sports history since 1985. Eric has written many sports books for adults and children, including the novels *Hockey Night in the Dominion of Canada* (Lester Publishing, 1992) and *Fever Season* (Dundurn Press, 2009). Eric is a member of the Society for International Hockey Research and the Society for American Baseball Research. Visit Eric's website at ericzweig.com

Index

New York Rangers.

Zweig, Eric
vjnfi
$27.60